COMEDIANS

**GEORGE BURNS   GEORGE CARLIN   BILLY CRYSTAL   WHOOPI GOLDBERG   BOB HOPE   ALAN KING
SAM KINISON   ROBERT KLEIN   JERRY LEWIS   RICHARD LEWIS   STEVE MARTIN   JACKIE MASON
RICHARD PRYOR   JOAN RIVERS   LILY TOMLIN   ROBIN WILLIAMS   STEVEN WRIGHT**

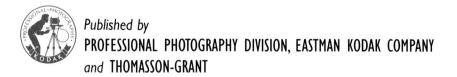

Published by
PROFESSIONAL PHOTOGRAPHY DIVISION, EASTMAN KODAK COMPANY
and THOMASSON-GRANT

COMEDIANS

ARTHUR GRACE

Published by the
Professional Photography Division, Eastman Kodak Company
and Thomasson-Grant, Inc.

Designed by Alex Castro
Photographs edited by Jane Livingston
Production prints by Bill Pierce

Printed in the United States of America by Garamond/Pridemark.

97 96 95 94 93 92 91   5 4 3 2 1

Library of Congress Cataloging-in-Publication Data
Grace, Arthur.
      Comedians / Arthur Grace.
          p.   cm.
      ISBN 0-934738-80-7 (hardbound) -- ISBN 0-934738-92-0
(softbound)
      1. Comedians--United States--Portraits. 2. Comedians--United
States--Quotations.   I. Title.
      PN2285.G69   1991
      792.7' 028' 092273--dc20
      [B]   91-21465
                                                            CIP

Thomasson-Grant, Inc.
One Morton Drive, Suite 500
Charlottesville, Virginia 22901
(804) 977-1780

Contents

Introduction

I'm sure there's a lot of truth in Edmund Gwenn's quip, although what really amazes me is how anyone can manage to say something amusing on his deathbed. I'd be having other people humor me, not vice versa. Nevertheless, in my own small way, I do relate to the very real difficulty of doing comedy. Only a handful of people may remember, but in August 1968, for one week only, I took the stage as the "Sky Pilot."

During that summer, a friend of mine was running a church-sponsored coffeehouse on Cape Cod, and as part of the deal, he was given a large, rent-free house. Since I needed a place to stay, it was decided that in exchange for a free room, I would become the resident comedian at the coffeehouse, filling in between folk singers. I outfitted myself at an Army-Navy surplus store with an

6

orange flight suit, leather flying helmet, and rose-colored prism glasses, and fueled to the gills for my maiden flight, I flew into the world of stand-up comedy.

The crowd I faced on opening night was heavily fogged in from recreational drugs of one sort or another (and I wasn't doing much better from the control tower), but somehow I got them laughing for 20 minutes, telling some convoluted story of a camping trip I'd taken to the Great Smoky Mountains. It felt great when I came off stage to what seemed like thunderous applause. But then it hit me. I was going to have to do the same thing again in an hour—first time lucky, but there was no way I was going to try to be funny on a regular basis. I struggled through the rest of the week with modest success (depending on my body rhythms) then hitchhiked to Staten Island on my night off and never returned.

It wasn't until 18 years later, as a staff photographer for *Newsweek*, that I once again became involved with stand-up comedy. Mercifully, it was only as an observer assigned to shoot a cover story on Robin Williams. During the time I traveled with him around the country as he completed his concert tour, I was constantly amazed, not only by his talent, but by his professionalism. Night after night, regardless of his mood or how the day had gone, he stepped out in front of 3,000 people and gave them their money's worth with a high-energy display of comedy pyrotechnics.

I remember one rainy morning we woke up early in Blacksburg, Virginia, and took a dreary one-hour van ride to the airport. After a half-hour wait for a delayed flight, we boarded a twin-engine cigar tube with no standing headroom and no toilet for an hour-and-thirty-minute flight to Cleveland. None of us could wait to get off and connect to our jet flight to Milwaukee. As soon as we landed, we were escorted by airline personnel across the tarmac toward a beautiful 727. We were in shock as we were led past the gangway and under the belly of the jet toward another toilet-less, food-less, and drink-less propeller-driven cigar tube. Everyone gritted their teeth and sullenly boarded the commuter special for the 90-minute bladder rattler to Milwaukee.

Later that afternoon, still gloomy, we drove from the airport in silence, feeling like part of a funeral procession, which is probably why David Steinberg, Robin's manager, happened to mention that an elderly gentleman they both knew in the entertainment business had passed away the day before. "Ah, death," Robin shot back instantly, "Nature's way of saying, 'Check, please!'" That was it. The ice was broken, the laughs started coming, and Robin went on to do two great sold-out shows that night.

Over the next few years, I encountered Robin from time to time, and as a result, I met more and more comedians. It was in April 1989 at a rehearsal for Comic Relief in Los Angeles that the idea first occurred to me to do a book on comedians. I was sitting around backstage listening to a group of producers and managers with long years of experience in the comedy business discuss stand-up comedians, both past and present. They were having plenty of laughs, but at the same time, there was an unmistakable aura of respect and affection for the performers they were rating and evaluating.

When I thought about it later, it seemed to me that comedians were underappreciated and underrated as artists. It's the old conundrum—if it's funny, how can it be taken seriously? For whatever reason, comedy is perceived as "lightweight," of somehow lacking intellectual throw weight, when compared with some of the other arts. In doing a book on stand-up comedians, my idea was to single them out as a group of artists deserving of special attention and recognition. The way I see it, theirs is an extraordinary talent married to a high-risk and unforgiving job.

How difficult is it to do stand-up comedy? Listen to Bernie Brillstein, chairman of Brillstein-Grey Productions in Los Angeles. "You see these comedians backstage, and you have a drink with them. And then it's, 'And now ladies and gentlemen …' Forget it! If I had to do that, I'd be in the dressing room with diarrhea. It's like matadors. Man, if you do stand-up comedy, you're facing failure every moment you're out there."

Usually stand-up comedians are equipped with nothing more than a microphone when they walk out alone to face an audience, whether it's 30 drunks in a smoke-filled club or 3,000 adoring fans in a darkened auditorium. Their job is to keep them laughing for an hour or more, relying totally on themselves, using their wit, intelligence, and whatever else they can call upon to pull it off. And unlike an actor or musician who waits until the curtain comes down or the last note has been played to find out how he's done, stand-ups usually know if they're hitting or missing every ten or fifteen seconds. It's immediate, it's live, and it's spontaneous, and that's the rush for those who perform stand-up. They get instant gratification or instant rejection. As Bud Friedman, founder of the Improv comedy club, puts it, "This is what they do for a living, audition every night of their life."

For many comedians, it's worth it, because stand-up also provides these individualistic and independent performers something else that they prize: total control over their show and complete responsibility for its outcome. Of course, when things don't go well, it's a little difficult for a stand-up to come off stage and start blaming his costars and his director. Stand-ups generally write alone, work alone, and get the laughter and applause alone. And that's the way they like it.

Another interesting element sets stand-up apart from other stage performances, such as plays, ballets, and symphonies, which have clearly defined, predetermined endings. With stand-up, you never know exactly how and when the show will end, and a lot of comedians seem fascinated by that. "It's like a ritual," explains Steven Wright, "and it doesn't end until you come off. No matter what happens. If they're going crazy, if it's going bad, if it's going up and down, it won't end until you walk off. It's the only way it can end … even if 1,900 people left."

People walking out on comedians or tuning out comedy isn't a problem these days. America's appetite for stand-up has seemed insatiable in recent years. According to Bud Friedman, when he opened the Improv 28 years ago, there were no comedy clubs and maybe 100 comics nationwide. Now, he estimates, there are over 300 comedy clubs and thousands of comics throughout the country. Many experts in the field attribute the explosion in comedy to cable television, which for the first time allowed a nationwide audience to view a complete, uncensored performance by a comedian instead of the abridged versions that had long been seen on network variety and talk shows. Also, the simultaneous increase in the number of comedy clubs allowed large numbers of new comedians to be able to work.

Others in the comedy business see things from the perspective of basic economics. "Somebody discovered—probably Bud Friedman—that it was inexpensive to have one microphone and a handful of comedians who got up and entertained people for an evening," suggests Los Angeles film producer and manager Larry Brezner. "All of a sudden, the need for a variety show was gone. It was good enough to laugh for an hour."

"There's a big difference between being the funniest guy in your high school and making it on the stage. There's a big difference between cocktail party funny and professional funny … about 20 grand a week."

—David Steinberg (Morr, Brezner, & Steinberg) 6/25/90

For young people in America, the boom of comedy on cable TV and in clubs meant that the thought of becoming a comedian wasn't so far-fetched any more; suddenly, it seemed just as reasonable a career aspiration as doctor or corporate raider. And why not? "You don't have to take piano lessons," points out Bernie Brillstein. "All you have to do is get up on stage and try, and maybe you can do it." According to Bud Friedman, it is not unusual these days for a 12-year-old kid to tell his parents that he wants to become a comedian. "And it's not because he's not getting enough attention. It's because he sees Robin Williams on cable and says, 'That man is enjoying himself, and I'm having a lot of fun watching him. It's better than my dad's job—he's a lawyer. I never see him on TV.'"

The problem for all these aspiring comedy stars is finding out whether they have the amalgam of personality traits and natural abilities required for success as a professional stand-up: intelligence, creativity, perseverance, ambition, desire, vulnerability, diligence, and courage. Of course, they have to come equipped with a sense of humor (often overlooked), but more importantly, they need a special gift—the ability to make people laugh whenever they want them to.

If you polled people in the business about what characteristics stand-ups seem to have in common, you'd find the adjective 'insecure' high on everybody's list. "Comedians live with insecurity," says Jack Rollins, the legendary manager of many of the biggest comedy stars in the last 40 years, among them Woody Allen, Elaine May, Robert Klein, Robin Williams, and David Letterman. "Insecurity seems to be the stuff of their comedy. That quality is very universal among comedians. I think it's what leads most of them into the business."

Recently I was having a conversation with a woman who is married to a professional stand-up, and we were talking about a friend of ours who had just started dating a comedian who tours the country. I expressed my apprehension and dismay that our friend, who was newly divorced and was looking for some solid footing, had gotten herself involved with a stand-up. "Yeah," my married friend agreed, "I can tell you for sure that comedians aren't the greatest catch in the world, but they're definitely one notch better than photojournalists or policemen."

She might be right, but at least as a photojournalist I'll never have to be exposed to the danger of "bombing" in front of an audience, a nightmare scenario that visits every stand-up comedian. It can happen to anyone on any given night, but obviously, the younger comedians bomb (and must deal with it psychologically) most often. One night I was sitting in Sam Kinison's dressing room in upstate New York talking to a few young comedians who happened to be opening for Sam. One of them had just come off stage after doing his 20 minutes and was telling the others how the crowd was. After hearing that everything was great out there, another comedian who was about to go on nervously lit a cigarette and, almost in a trance, told a story of what had happened to him six months earlier.

He was opening for a headliner at a packed venue in Long Island, and for some reason the mood of the crowd was incredibly ugly. They'd just booed a local rock band off the stage, and when he came on, he fared no better. In no time at all, they started heckling him, then shouting him down, then booing him. He used his best put-downs to try to regain control, but that only riled the crowd even more. Some people started to rush the stage, and watching the nightmare unfold in slow motion right before his eyes, he was suddenly whisked out of harm's way by some alert security guards. As he told the story, he kept taking quick, deep drags on his cigarette and staring blankly at the floor, obviously not quite over the experience.

"Nobody likes to bomb, and nobody wants to see anybody bomb, but it does happen," says Buddy Morra, Billy Crystal's manager. "It's a process sometimes. Hopefully, you learn from the bombing. And that takes you to the next level, gets you there."

But getting there and staying there are two different things, and no comedian stays on top without hard work and good material. Nothing seems to anger comedians more than watching other comedians who don't give it 100 percent on stage, who put it on autopilot, or "phone it in." As Jerry Lewis states unequivocally, "The thing that drives me insane is the performer who goes out and dogs it."

In the end, no matter how much time comedians devote to working on their acts and regardless of the energy they put into their stage performances, material is the key to success or failure. Young comedians who struggle to build up an act are in awe of the sheer volume of material produced over the years on albums and in HBO specials by the likes of Richard Pryor, Bill Cosby, George Carlin, and Robert Klein, or of someone like Jackie Mason, who has written and starred in back-to-back, one-man Broadway shows.

A few years ago I was sitting in my office at Newsweek waiting to meet an insurance agent. When he walked in, he said a quick hello and headed straight over to my bulletin board to check out some photographs. He asked me if I had taken the pictures of Robin Williams, and when I said yes, he immediately sat down and told me that he used to be a stand-up comedian himself. He went on to describe how he had played the local comedy club circuit and eventually emceed on weekends for New York City headliners. He said he still remembered his act and asked me if I wanted to hear it. I said sure (starting to feel as if I were in a Woody Allen movie). There were some very funny lines while it lasted.

When I asked him to keep going, he look dejectedly over at the bulletin board and then back at me. "That's the problem why I never made it," he said. "I only had a good ten minutes."

Throughout the 15 months I worked on this book, I heard hours and hours of brilliant material from the comedians included in these pages, and I know it took them years to create and develop that material, as well as their own individual styles. Still, I'm sure there are a lot of people who are asking themselves why such-and-such comedian, who is incredibly talented and funny, isn't in this book.

First of all, for this project I was only interested in comedians who are well known as stand-ups, although they may not be performing stand-up at the present time. No sketch or ensemble comedians, or comic actors, were considered. Certain other comedians are missing simply because they said, for whatever reason, that they didn't want to be in the book. For instance, four comedians were planning to do their own books. Several others wanted to be paid (nobody was compensated), while Henny Youngman, instead of being photographed, wanted to sell me pictures of himself with all the big stars over the years. Every time I was set to photograph Roseanne Barr, she seemed to change publicists or managers. And when I finally had a good friend of hers ready to make a phone call on my behalf, Roseanne sang the national anthem in San Diego that very night.

It took me six weeks and over 20 phone calls to get in touch with one of Eddie Murphy's people. When I finally got through to him on the phone and had my 60 seconds to pitch the book, he quickly said no to my first two reasons why I felt Eddie would want to do the book. In one last attempt, I pointed out to him that one of the primary goals of the book was to produce a visual, historical record of comedic artists in 1990. He instantly shot back that Eddie couldn't care less about history, said no for the final time, and hung up.

A few other facts about the making of this book may be useful to the reader. The quotations included in the following pages were selected from taped conversations I had with each of the comedians. I hope that none of their words sound arrogant. I was asking them leading questions that called for honest, yet immodest, responses—like, what did you bring to comedy that wasn't there before you came on the scene, or how do you account for your success. Finally,

it's important to point out that *no* photographs were set up, and no comedian was ever posed or prompted in any way. What you see is exactly the way it was.

When I finished the book, there was one question that remained for me, and it might occur to the reader as well—What separates the many good comedians from the few truly great ones? Jack Rollins tried to explain it to me one afternoon in his office at the Letterman show: "The greats all have individuality and personal distinction. They are not interchangeable with other comedians either because of style, or personality, or both. They have an incisiveness to illuminate a corner in people's consciousness that they have been feeling. And when they do put a flashlight on that little thing, whatever that may be, the feeling is, 'Oh yeah, oh yeah, that's right. Now it's defined. He's seen it as I have felt it.'" In a final and very revealing comment, he added, "It's not so much what a comedian does on stage, it's what remains on stage after the comedian's left."

To many of us, stand-up comedy has a special place in the arts, but one that's difficult to define and articulate. Maybe for now, we'll just have to go with Larry Brezner's assessment: "When you've laughed at comedians who are one of a kind," he observes, "then that experience is more than simply the stand-up comedy experience. It's seeing Picasso painting live."

—*Arthur Grace*

COMEDIANS

To my friends Marsha and Robin, who started it all....
and to my wife Florence, who saw me through to the finish (again).

George Burns

"NO, I'M NOT NERVOUS [right before going on stage]. When I worked with Gracie, Gracie got nervous. To get nervous, you gotta have a lot of talent, and Gracie had the talent."

"At my age, it's very hard for me to stand up for an hour. But if you walk out on the stage and the audience loves you, it gives you a lot of energy. If the audience likes it, I give a great performance. If the audience don't like it, I still give a great performance. The audience are very glad to see me. They say, 'How do you like that, he walks!' "

"I love show business. I love show business as much today as I did when I first started. I'm very lucky to be in show business. To be 94 and get out of bed in the morning and love what you're going to do that day is very important."

I first photographed George Burns at his office on the old Hollywood General Studios lot in Los Angeles. It was the same office he'd been in since 1950 when he and Gracie were doing their TV show, and it probably hadn't changed much since then. There was fake wood paneling on the walls, multicolored shag carpeting on the floor, cool overhead fluorescent lighting, and freestanding ashtrays like you used to see in hotel lobbies and barbershops. George was busy signing copies of his latest bestseller, *All My Best Friends*, and reading *Variety*. At exactly 11:45 A.M., he got up from his desk, said goodbye, and walked to the door. It was time for his assistant to drive him to Hillcrest Country Club for lunch and his bridge game.

About six weeks later, I happened to call Irving Fein, George's manager, to check on dates when I could photograph George performing. He told me that George was going to fill in for the Judds at Caesar's Palace that weekend. I flew out to Las Vegas the next day and witnessed something truly amazing on Saturday night, March 10, 1990—George Burns at age 94 doing back-to-back one-hour shows in the Circus Maximus room.

He arrived in his dressing room backstage around 8:00 P.M. and left about 1:15 A.M. In between, he received two standing ovations from adoring audiences, had a few martinis, ate a toasted bagel with cream cheese, smoked cigars, drank some coffee, and chatted with old friends.

It was during one of these backstage visits that I learned something new about George Burns. Someone offered him an expensive Cuban cigar, and George politely declined. The man persisted. "But George, it's Cuban, the best. You'll love it. C'mon, take it."

"I don't want it," repeated Burns. "I'll tell you what kind of cigars I smoke. The three-for-a-dollar kind. If I get any of those ten-dollar ones, I give them to Danny Thomas. I like El Productos, and you know why? Because an expensive cigar is rolled tight, but a cheap one is very loose. When I put my cigar in a holder, the expensive ones go out all the time. I need my cigar to keep burning the whole time I'm on stage. That's why I always smoke the three-for-a-dollar kind."

Just before he went up to his room after the second show, two actors from the show *La Cage Aux Folles* stopped by the dressing room to have George sign a poster. "Oh, Mr. Burns," one of them said in awe, "I hope I make it to 94." George looked him right in the eye and replied, "Don't worry, kid. Just keep loving what you're doing, and you'll get there."

As we walked through the kitchen area to get to the hotel elevators, I said goodnight to George and thanked him for letting me photograph him. All he said was, "I hope your book's a smash, kid."

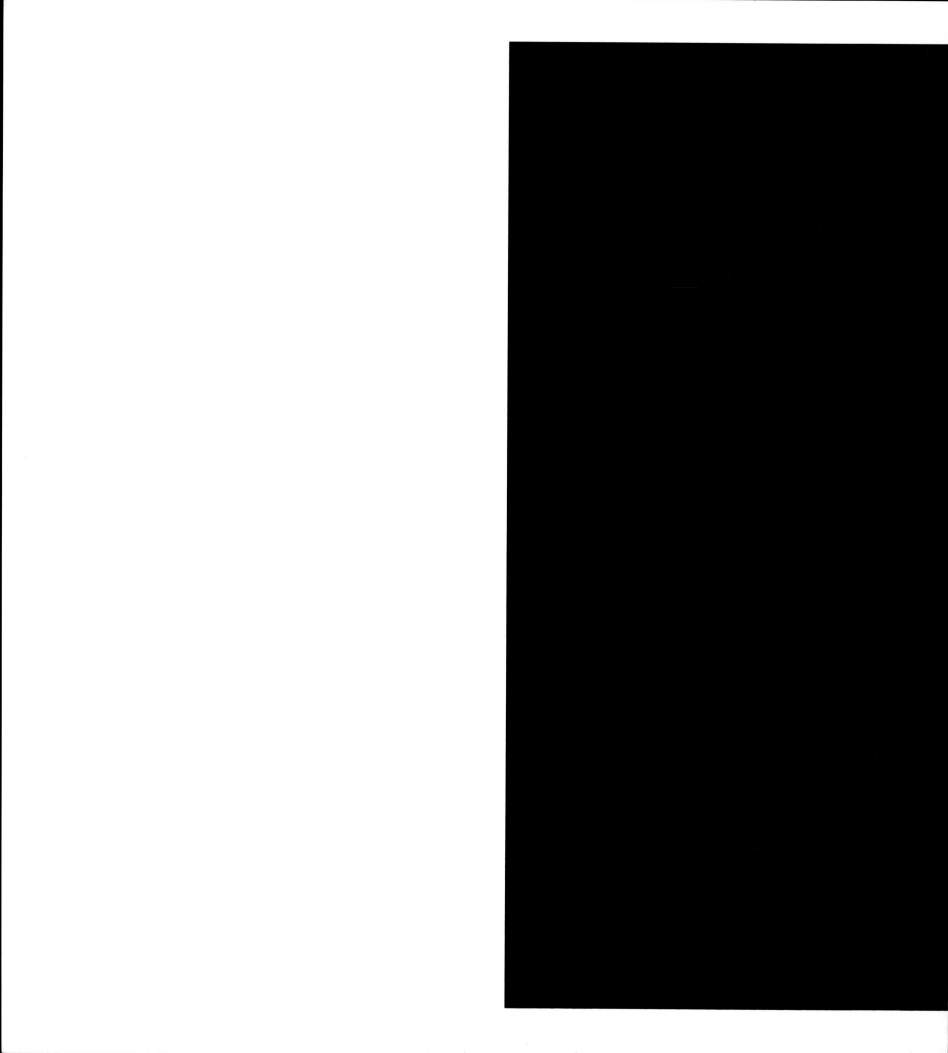

George Carlin

George Carlin is a man who loves his work—he does about 120 dates a year crisscrossing the country performing in a variety of venues from college gymnasiums to theaters to Las Vegas showrooms. He has a "use it or lose it" philosophy about stand-up comedy—you have to keep working at it, or you lose your ability to do it well. "You can practice the violin alone, but you can't practice comedy alone," he says. "You have to be out in front of audiences."

I finally caught up with George over a late April weekend when he was based in Manhattan for two nearby college concert dates at Suffolk Community College in Selden, New York, and Monmouth College in West Long Branch, New Jersey.

We got off to an inauspicious start the afternoon I met him to ride out to Long Island. No sooner had we pulled away from his hotel than the stretch limo we were riding in sputtered and stalled in the middle of rush hour in front of the Plaza Hotel. It was unseasonably hot, around 90 degrees, and the driver, George, and I all hopped out to push our ride to the side of the street while horns honked and people stared. George never broke a sweat, and sat back drinking a diet soda as the driver called for another car. His only concern seemed to be reassuring the driver that it wasn't his fault and that he shouldn't worry.

Over the course of the weekend, I had a chance to watch George in his performing mode. Before the show, he talks to anybody and everybody (police, students, promoters, caterers), always polite and approachable. But he never sits still and is like a coiled spring. He takes a few minutes right before he goes on stage to collect his thoughts, and then boom, he delivers a physically demanding and mentally exhausting hour and 20 minutes of nonstop, original Carlin humor. After the show, it's exit stage left and into a waiting car.

I saw George again at the end of May when he was in Manhattan doing promotion for his record seventh HBO special ("Doin' It Again"). It was one of those grueling press whirlwinds with early morning talk show appearances, print interviews in the hotel suite, MTV tapings, and late-night talk radio programs. After more than three decades in the comedy business—with its ups and downs, ins and outs, fads and trends—here George was, still in demand, with his passion and unique point of view intact. He remarked to me that day that people who see his show are either repelled by it or invited in. It reminded me of the joke George tells about a new cockroach spray. It doesn't kill the cockroaches, it just fills them with self-doubt about whether they're in the right house or not.

"THE THING ABOUT STAND-UP that makes it special is that it is a solo, high-wire act. You're looking for approval every five, ten, or fifteen seconds, and you're trying to sustain that approval from moment to moment to moment. You're constantly testing. You're unzipping your soul. You're putting everything on the line, saying, 'Here's what I consider intelligent. Here's what I consider funny. What do you people think?'"

"No one is ever more him- or herself than at the moment they are laughing. It is like a perfect Zen moment of letting go of the world. Right at the point when the joke hits your brain and your brain understands it, all defenses are down. And it is at a moment like that when a new idea can best be implanted."

"It seems to me that of all the artists there are—poets, painters, sculptors—the stand-up comedian is the only one who gets to create the work in front of the people it's intended for, allows the people to shape the work through their reaction at the time it's being made."

"I don't like the time before the show, because you're going to do something and it's not happening yet. I'm sort of a blank, because I want to get out there and start living moment to moment. When I'm standing back there, I have 90 minutes ahead of me. When I'm on the stage, I only have ten seconds ahead of me."

"After I'm finished I don't like to hang around the building. I just want to get away. I just want to go and live the next hour. I like to get into the next part of my life. I'm in the car, I'm moving, the radio's on—life has started again."

"The public has no idea, people who are interested in comedy have no idea, how painstaking a process it is to get material together, to do five minutes or whatever, and how it separates the great comics from the ones who never made it, the also-rans."

Billy Crystal

I worked with Billy Crystal in Los Angeles in late January 1990 during the few days he was doing promotional and other activities for his duties as host of the Oscar telecast in March. We went from magazine cover shoots to ABC promo tapings, from Oscar production meetings to tuxedo fittings at Armani in Beverly Hills.

The only problem we had was when Billy put sunglasses on the giant Oscars that were being used as promotional props. He had his shades on and was straddling the two eight-foot, Ray-Ban-decked-out statues when the publicist from the academy happened to walk in. He was nearly choking in shock as he screamed, "Stop! Stop! You can't do that!" We explained that we were just having some fun and that the pictures were only for personal use, not publication. He calmed down somewhat, but later that night a messenger delivered an envelope to my hotel from the academy. It included a warning letter about defacing the Oscar and the rule book for the 62nd Annual Academy Awards.

A few weeks later, we met again at a resort outside Phoenix where Billy was performing in concert. The night we all arrived, we had to kill some time in the back of the limousine while the driver went in to register everybody and get the room keys. That's where I witnessed my first "Sammy-Off," which is when David Steinberg, Billy's manager, and whoever else happens to be nearby, challenge Billy to see who can do the best Sammy Davis, Jr. impersonation. Watching three amateurs in a confined space simultaneously trying to out-"Sammy" Billy was a scene right out of "The Gong Show."

The next day everybody played nine holes of golf (more or less) and then waited around the rooms until showtime. Later that evening as Billy was being escorted to the stage through the kitchen area, two teenaged waitresses approached him for an autograph. Billy was happy to oblige, but no sooner had he finished signing when one of the girls blurted out, "Gee, I thought you'd be taller!" Billy just kept walking toward the stage and talking to himself: "Thanks a lot. I really needed that. Just the ego boost I needed before I go on. Where do I send the check?" The continuing monologue with himself was as funny as anything he said on stage all night. (A year later, I mentioned the incident to Billy. "Sure, I remember it," he laughed, "it was like a Scud right into my ego.")

"THERE IS AN ART TO DOING WHAT WE DO—let's see, that's like saying Michelangelo and Jackie Mason in the same sentence. I think it's an ancient art that goes back to the first cave drawings—the first one was of a man giving a woman to a ravenous Tyrannosaurus, and that was, 'Take my wife, please!'"

"The comic on stage always controls his own destiny. You write, you produce, you direct, you do everything in that hour yourself. You're getting it instantly. You give it out to the audience. They laugh. They tell you right away, 'We like you,' or 'We don't like you.'"

"[Right before I go out on stage] it's just, let's do it. Deep breath, relax myself, and go have fun. I keep telling myself how lucky I am that I'm doing what I've wanted to do since I was a kid. I always feel that. Otherwise, I'm not quite sure where I am half the time."

"You can't bomb in a film while the film is going on. But the thing with stand-up is, there's nobody who comes out and goes—'Cut! Can we do it again?' You can never start over."

"[The night I hosted the Oscars] I kept thinking, this is amazing, and tried to remember the monologue, because you don't rehearse it. You write it and then you do it. And you'd better be great. And you walk out there and you know you're not doing your act that you could kill them with in a second. You're doing special material just written for that night that you'll never do again. It's as it goes. That's it. It's dangerous."

"I'm not the best jokesmith in the world, but what I've tried to bring is a sense of style and a sense of someone who can say things in a funny and serious and touching way. I've tried to show that you don't have to yell to be heard."

Whoopi Goldberg

I started photographing Whoopi Goldberg when she was in New York to co-host Comic Relief. It was a hectic five days for her, involving writing, rehearsing, and promoting the show. The highlight of the week (other than Whoopi's high-kicking number with the Rockettes) was watching her get kissed by various baseball stars before the Mets-Dodgers game at Comic Relief night at Shea Stadium.

The next time I saw her was in July at a high school in Los Angeles where she was filming "Hot Rod Brown, Class Clown" for the Nickelodeon series, "Tales from the Whoop." During one of the breaks in filming, I sat down with Whoopi and a few of her friends in her trailer and watched parts of "Comic Relief" on her VCR. She'd been so busy the night of the show that she hadn't seen most of it. Afterward, I asked her how she develops her material and goes through the process of weeding out what works from what doesn't.

Whoopi feels you can't just go right to the Comedy Store or the Improv to try out new material. She likes to work the small rooms in Las Vegas because you get a wider range of people. "You get everybody," she says. "You get nuns, you get traveling midgets on horseback, you get everything. And after three or four nights, you know if the material is strong enough to stand. And you can do it anywhere, and it doesn't kill you."

I finished up my pictures with Whoopi in October on a return trip to Los Angeles. It was a busy time for her. We went from the set of "Bagdad Cafe" to the "Motown 30th Anniversary Special" at the Pantages Theater in Hollywood (where Whoopi did a hilarious spoof of Diana Ross to open the show) to a photo shoot for *Vogue* in a plush studio overlooking Sunset Strip (with Whoopi wearing a red-hot, skintight, midthigh Gianni Versace number).

One night she received a humanitarian award from Women in Show Business. It was a memorable evening because I got to watch singer Little Anthony bring the house down and then Pia Zadora put it to sleep. She set a new world record for unsolicited encores. Whoopi sat stoically throughout until, sometime around midnight, she was finally called to come up to the podium to receive her award (which at that point should have come with a campaign ribbon and a Purple Heart). Whoopi stepped up to the microphone and began, "It's wonderful to be here tonight. Or is it tomorrow? And I want to thank Pia for her singing...and singing."

"COMEDY IS SO SUBJECTIVE. You go out on stage, and you either eat it or you don't. And it's brutal. I've seen great people die brutally. Yeah, I've died brutally. Yeah, I've eaten it brutally. It's just like, woah, I'm never doing this again. But you always have to keep in mind that you're going to have good days and bad days and not all material works for all audiences."

"I love watching funny people who are having a good time [on stage] because as an audience person, I want to see that you enjoy what you're doing. If you're having fun, so will I."

"What goes through my mind [ten seconds before I go out on stage] is I should be working at Bank of America. That's the last thing I think of, B. of A."

"They're always up for you when you come out. After the first half is when you know—I should have stayed in the room."

"Longevity is talent. You only last if you have some talent. I believe I do. People look at me and say, 'Well, if you did it, I can certainly do it.' I'm like the kid next door who made good. It's sort of like people go to see what their sister's doing."

"We're in a world where men decide who is going to make it. So if you don't fit some guy's criteria of what a funny woman is supposed to be, then you don't get on. No, you don't make it."

"I've always felt like there might be a different way to look at things. I've always tried to make that the essence of my work—my comedy work—simply because I always think it's important for people to have two or three different ways to look at stuff, not that they have to agree, and I'm not necessarily out to change anybody's mind. It's just the way that I am."

"I hope that comedy remains open and fun and loose and free, and that people remember tolerance lest it come back and eat them."

Bob Hope

"I'VE KNOWN ALL THE COMEDIANS right on down through the years from the time I started in the early twenties, and I'd watched them in vaudeville. Jack Benny was very popular, so I tried to sort of emulate him. Then I found a fast thing, like doing jokes like Walter Winchell talked. I talked very fast, and the audience had to catch up with me. It sort of flattered their intelligence. This speed style, it really worked. And they're doing it today quite a bit now, running away from the punch line."

Although Bob Hope doesn't perform in concert that often anymore, I did have a chance to photograph him doing this type of classic stand-up comedy when he appeared at the Orange Pavilion in San Bernardino, California, for a National Guard group.

He arrived by limousine late in the afternoon, said hello to his hosts, greeted a few well-wishers, had a brief photo op with the local press, then proceeded to the pavilion for rehearsal. Immediately afterward he headed straight for his car. Just before he got in, Ward Grant, his publicist, introduced me to Bob, who told me that he was going back to his hotel room to rest up before the show because he was getting over a bad cold and didn't feel well. He also confided in a mischievous tone that he needed to go over his material since he hadn't performed in concert in over five months and was a bit rusty.

He returned later that evening, about ten minutes before he was scheduled to go on stage. Heading directly to the backstage area, he looked around for a moment and then walked into a utility closet to study his notes one last time. He emerged in a couple of minutes and sat down alone in the dark on a folding chair, waiting for his introduction. All of a sudden, a police officer appeared out of nowhere, shined a light right into Hope's face, and gruffly demanded to know what he was doing

there. Instantly realizing his mistake, he gushed, "Gee, it's Bob Hope. Hey, can I have your autograph?" It was just then that Hope's name was announced over the PA system, so while the security man held the flashlight, Hope scribbled his name and hurried for the stage.

The show went smoothly, the jokes had a slight shade of blue that you don't hear on network TV, and the adoring audience gave Hope a rousing ovation. After taking a few bows, he posed briefly with local beauty queens, signed some autographs, and was whisked off into the night in his limo.

About a month later, Bob was in Washington for a dinner benefit and a press conference before leaving for Berlin and points east to tape a TV special. I arranged to meet him in his hotel suite early in the afternoon for a brief interview. Somehow we got on the subject of golf, and he pulled a gold money clip from his pocket. It had a diamond in the center and engraved on it was, "PGA 1942." He told me that the Professional Golfers Association had presented one to him and one to Bing Crosby that year.

Seeing the clip triggered a question I was asking all the comedians: "Do you think comedians are the poor relations of the acting business?"

"They're not the poor relations," he laughed. "Most of the comedians I know are plenty loaded."

"I imitated Chaplin when I was a kid in New York. Oh yeah, I did Chaplin, the whole thing. I saw him get out of a car on 44th Street and said, 'God, that's Chaplin.' I thought he was near God. I watched him and waited an hour until he came out of the building so I could look at him again."

"Stand-up is a matter of education and knowing how to pace yourself, change of material and everything else. You learn as you go along."

"I just clear my throat [before I go on stage] and try to open my mouth and sing a little bit, that's all. Because nothing goes through your mind unless you're trying to remember something that's topical that happened. See, when you do it as long as George Burns or I have done it, there is so much we can do. There is so much up here that you have in your head, you can meet almost any situation. You just go. You don't worry about it."

"You feel better when you come off stage than you do when you go on. I do. Because it wakes everything up. You're thinking and everything. The laughs. There's nothing like laughs, you know. When I go to the golf club and there's a bunch of guys, I go right over and say, 'What's goin' on?' I mean, I want to hear that joke."

Alan King

"I'VE ALWAYS CONSIDERED MYSELF a blue-collar worker in an art form. Standing out there for an hour making people laugh, if that's not an art form, I don't know what is."

"The best advice I ever got—when I was a kid I remember meeting Bob Hope, and I said to Bob, 'Have you got any advice?' He said to me, 'Remember kid, nobody ever got discovered laying off. You've got to work. You don't get better laying off.'"

"I'm a professional. I've been doing it so long it's almost second nature. You wake me up in the middle of the night, I can do 40 minutes. It's what I do."

"[Before I go on stage] I pump myself up like an athlete— emotionally, mentally. It's like a surgeon. I mean, these people come to see me and pay this kind of money, it can't be hit and miss. You know, you don't go to a surgeon and say this was an off day for him."

In late May 1990, I took a train out to Long Island to photograph Alan King at Westbury Music Fair where he was booked for a five-day concert engagement. I arrived late in the afternoon because I wanted to be in time for his sound check and run-through. By the time I cleared in with theater management and had a union rules briefing (no photography allowed in the theater unless you could come up with $500 for the electrician), I really needed a laugh.

Alan had arrived even earlier than I and was already ensconced on the couch in his dressing room making telephone calls while his clothes and show materials were being attended to by his assistant. Over the next several hours, Alan changed from his casual clothes to his lounging robe and finally into his tuxedo. There seemed to be a kind of ritualistic rhythm to all of this. Alan is from a generation of performers who have an aversion to putting on their tux pants until just before they go on stage (which is why I wound up photographing a lot of them in their boxer shorts).

During all this time, Alan had a few cups of coffee, smoked some cigars, nursed a couple of Tanquerays over ice, chatted with friends who dropped by, and studied his notes for the show. Everything he intended to do that night was jotted down on one page of a yellow legal pad. He explained to me that what he'd written were keys to get him going and give him continuity, and they would become an hour-and-ten-minute show once he got on stage.

Later that evening, after all the congratulatory visits to his dressing room by friends, relatives, and management types, I asked Alan why he didn't do more concert dates since he seemed to enjoy it so much. He talked about all the demands on his time with his many business projects and obligations. Then he looked wistfully in my direction and said, "You know why I love to perform? Because it's the only peace and quiet I get these days—no phone calls, no messages, no problems. You know, for somebody like me, the stage is a very restful place."

"[After the show] if it went well, I'm elated. I feel good. There's a tiredness. It's physical out there, to stand up there. I get more exercise on the stage in an hour than I do all week. But, no, it's a job well done, what I've been paid for."

"I kind of undress for them [the audience]. I expose myself to them—my emotions, my thinking, politically, intellectually. And in the very beginning, I was the first angry young man. When I was doing the Sullivan shows, I started taking on the airlines and the medical profession and the legal profession and the telephone company, and I became well known for that. I was the ombudsman. I was talking for them. Standing, waiting for my luggage, I heard a woman whose luggage was lost and doesn't know I'm even within 5,000 miles, I hear her saying, 'This is like an Alan King routine.'"

"You're standing up there alone. There's 2,000, 3,000 people loving you and adoring you. What's not to like? They're laughing at you. Man, it's very rewarding on many levels."

"I've done so many things. But it's like when somebody asks me what do I do: 'I'm a stand-up comedian, actually.' It's what I do. 'Good evening, ladies and gentlemen' paid all the bills and put all the kids through school."

Sam Kinison

Sam Kinison's tour bus was already parked by the hotel in Rochester, New York, when my taxi pulled up from the airport. He and his entourage had driven into town in a slick custom bus (with all the amenities—TV, VCR, stereo), which he uses for concert tours.

Sam's management people in L.A. told me that when I arrived I should call Sam's brother Bill, who was his road manager. I got through to him later in the afternoon and found out that everybody had gone to sleep around noon and that Sam wouldn't be getting up until an hour or so before the show. The way the tour usually worked was that they would finish a concert, meet people backstage for a while, get something to eat, then hit the road for the next city and drive all night. When they pulled into town the next morning, Sam would head right off to local radio stations to promote that night's show and wouldn't get to sleep until later in the morning.

When Sam finally arrived at the auditorium, he went straight to his dressing room and had his friend Sabrina (who is also in the show) do his makeup. A few minutes before showtime, Sabrina and her sister Milika emerged from their dressing room in their minimal black leather outfits with matching collars. Sam hooked them on their leashes, and off they strolled to the stage.

It was a fairly boisterous crowd, and they really went crazy for Sam's finale, when he gets the name and phone number of a local woman who's broken the heart of some guy in the audience. Sam then calls her up and "reprimands" her as the crowd goes berserk and cheers him on. The scene backstage afterward also had its moments, since most of the guests were strippers from a nearby club where Sam had spent the morning.

Later that night, after making a guest appearance at a local comedy club as a favor to the owner, Sam and company headed off in their bus for Poughkeepsie while I endured an eight-hour, breakdown-delayed rail trip aboard an Amtrak train without a food car. Sam didn't allow any outsiders to travel on his bus because of a hatchet job by a writer for a national magazine who had recently traveled with the group. Apparently there were some exaggerated references to "substance abuse," among other things.

When I was with Sam, nobody so much as had a beer. Sam proudly pointed out to me that he no longer allowed any alcohol or drugs on tour and that he'd never felt better. "Yeah, I've been sober for 34 days. But as a friend of mine says, they weren't all in a row."

"COMEDY IS REALITY. If you play real, then it will work. In the right bit, all you have to do is turn your head and react and you'll kill. You'll slay. You don't have to play anything big and slip on a banana and fart. 'We're doing a comedy so everybody act like an ass! Everybody make sure people get it. Joke ahead! Buckle up!'"

"There's something I learned in evangelism. When I was a preacher, my dad told me that if it doesn't excite you, it's not going to excite them. And I see a lot of comics eat it on that same theory. Because they are so used to the material, they are so used to what they do, that they expect the audience to roll over, and I think it takes more than that. I think you have to be surprised by your own material again, no matter how many times you do it. Comedy is a business with a lot of casualties because people lose that energy, they lose that excitement. They come out and tell their jokes and expect the material to do it. And man, you've got to hit it like a wall, like a tidal wave."

"You usually isolate an audience when you scream, [but] I think I took the element of rage and made it very comedic."

"What goes through my mind the last ten seconds [before I go on stage]? I'm usually staring at the girls. I'm going, I can't wait 'til the show's over. But I start getting psyched up about five to ten minutes before. You start getting into this enigma type of thing, like the tornado getting ready to hit Oklahoma."

"I'm exhausted [after I come off stage]. I put a lot of energy into my stuff, and I usually save it for the last ten or fifteen minutes. I really get pumped. It's like a fight. You save it for the last few rounds. The first thing I feel is scheeewww, it's over, I'm out of it, I survived another one. And then the next thing I do is come down and ask Bill what we did. What were the numbers, were we in the bonus round? And the only dread afterward is meeting radio contest winners."

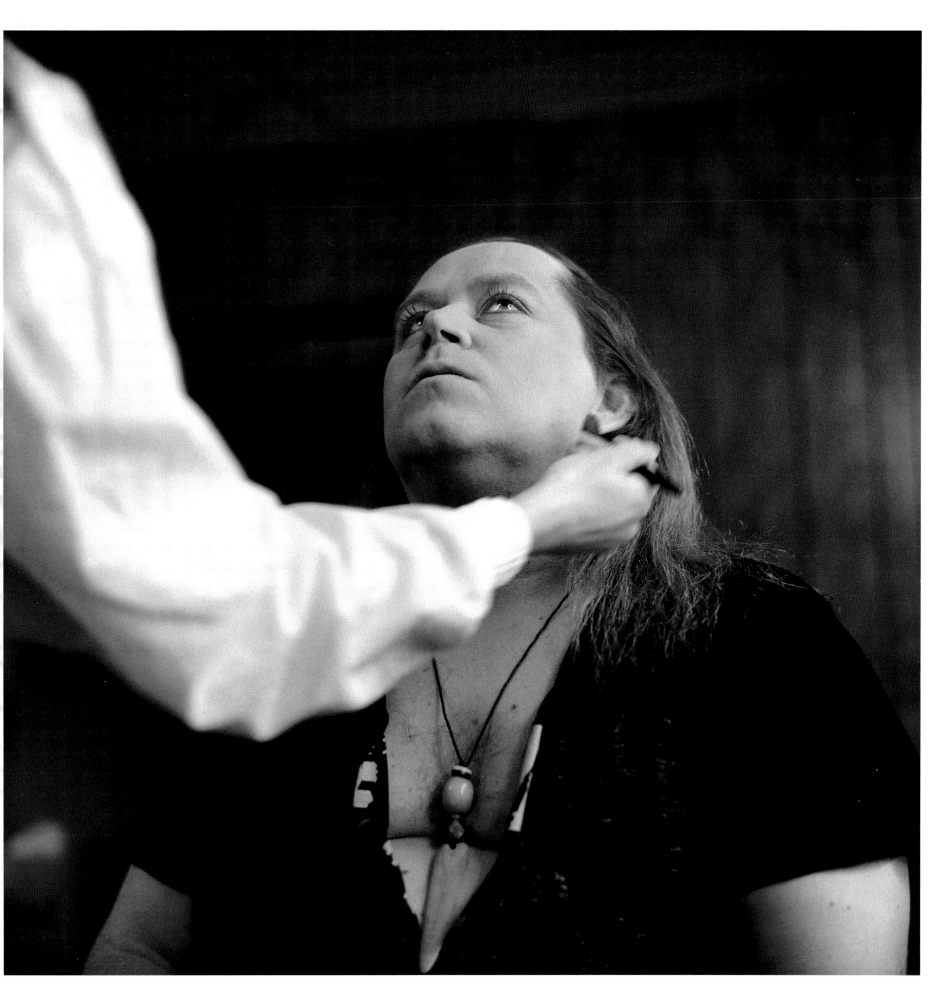

Robert Klein

"STAND-UP COMEDY is not really taught academically at major universities and things. You'll find a tremendous shortage of stand-up departments."

"I assume that most people who have become comedians were the class clown, the funny person at work. I have always held that the world is full of an enormous amount of stand-up talent. There are people at the post office who can make their friends scream. However, it is a quantum leap from doing it for friends or family or co-workers or whatever to doing it for strangers at a time and place of someone's choosing, on demand, for money."

"[Right before I walk out on stage] I think of an attack for the beginning. I can't go out there and languish. I can't think of many worse things, if you want to know the truth, than standing in front of an audience and bombing."

"I like the feeling when I come off stage much better than going on stage. You know, normally there's a reluctance to go on, a kind of, I don't know, almost like a dull dread, like I owe somebody something. But once I'm on stage, it's hard to get me off."

"What was important to me was conceptual comedy, not just a series of jokes, but impressions. I love silliness too. Funny is funny. I love the Three Stooges, but I always felt that if I could make a point too, that's delicious. That's something I'm proud of."

"Well, to make it in show business, period, you have to have desire. You have to have tenacity. You have to have balls of steel. You have to have nerve. You cannot sit quietly in the crowd and make it, especially as a comedian. I mean there is something daring about anyone who chooses to stand out by being funny. Making people laugh requires chance taking."

I first met Robert Klein on a rainy summer evening at Avery Fisher Hall in Manhattan. We both happened to arrive at the backstage entrance at the same time and introduced ourselves. Robert gave his name to the two guards who were seated at a monitoring station next to a bank of closed-circuit TVs. They looked blankly at one another and asked him again who he was. Robert politely explained that he was performing at that night's benefit. They huddled and decided that they'd better check with the talent coordinator, who quickly came downstairs and let us in. (I've heard from other comedians of Klein's stature that occasionally they've been refused entry to their own shows by some well-meaning security guard who only reads the sports pages.)

Klein shrugged off the episode as totally inconsequential and immediately launched into a litany of complaints about how his life was going at the time. He made the whole thing sound like a comedy routine, except he was living it.

He did a great 20 minutes to open the program, but as soon as he cleared the stage, he was back in his dressing room making calls to straighten out a few problems. Somehow, there was still a comedic element to all of it. When we left the building, the two guards by the door jumped up from behind their desk and enthusiastically greeted Robert. They told him how much they'd liked the show (they'd watched it on the closed-circuit monitor) and asked for his autograph. With a look of satisfaction, he obliged his two new fans and walked out to his car.

The next night we drove to Ft. Lee, New Jersey, where Robert was doing two shows at Bananas comedy club (located on weekends at the Holiday Inn). There was a long line already formed to get into the first show as we walked through the lobby and over to the elevators to go up to Robert's dressing room. Just at that moment, an older gentleman in line keeled over and fell to the floor, and people started yelling for an ambulance. As the elevator doors closed on the scene, Robert looked at me and deadpanned, "See, I knock 'em dead even before I get on stage."

The next time I saw Robert was in early October in New York where he was promoting his new video "Let's Not Make Love." He was doing a lot of radio and television as well as squeezing in an interview on comedy with a cable network at Catch A Rising Star. The following day Robert flew out to L.A. to do the "Tonight Show" and then red-eyed back to Washington, D.C., so he could perform that night with Marvin Hamlisch and others at the gala opening of George Mason University's new theater complex. Although he was jet-lagged, he seemed in fine fettle when I met him at his hotel room for the drive to the theater. There he was, looking distinguished in his black tie, but all I could think about was the image of him on Carson the night before, doing a hilarious bit on Yogi Berra standing nude in the locker room buffing his balls with a towel.

Jerry Lewis

When I finally connected with Jerry Lewis at TropWorld in Atlantic City, he was standing around on the showroom stage in shorts and a football jersey, rehearsing with his accompanist and the orchestra and schmoozing with singer Bobby Vinton.

We met again early that evening in Jerry's dressing room, which had an inner sanctum that was set up with the precision of a surgical operating room. Neatly hanging on a portable coatrack were six identical $2,000 tuxedos, each with the red insignia of the French Legion of Honor in their lapels. Duplicate pairs of black leather boots were nearby on the floor. Jerry said he would decide right before showtime which of the six tuxes he would wear that evening.

Arrayed on the countertop in front of the makeup mirror were pens, notepaper, personal photographs, cough drops, throat spray, three pairs of underwear, three pairs of socks, nail clippers, scissors, and brushes. There were also assorted cassette tapes of previous shows (he tapes every performance) labeled with the time they ran and how good the shows were. The four I saw read "Stupendous," "Superb," "Super," and "Super Good," but Jerry was quick to point out he had a few back home labeled "Hiroshima."

I asked Jerry what he brought to comedy that wasn't there before he came on the scene. "Insanity," he answered immediately. "Childlike, nine years old, because that's all I am. An abandon, silliness, no shame, anything goes to give them pleasure. I took the nine-year-old that got laughs in my class and turned it into pay dirt. And that's why my next birthday when I'm 65, I'm gonna be nine again."

"There's two of you, the 64-year-old and the nine-year-old?" I asked.

He nodded. "And the 64-year-old," he went on, "must do everything he possibly can to make the nine-year-old comfortable so that he can go out on that stage and make his living."

"But you also said that when you—when the nine-year-old's on stage, you leave the 64-year-old in the dressing room."

"Oh, he's in the dressing room, absolutely. Definitely."

"And then when you come back from on stage . . ."

"Then the 64-year-old will pass judgment on the nine-year-old's performance. He'll say either 'Bravo' or 'Practice, schmuck!'"

"And that's the end of the nine-year-old?"

"That's it," he replied. "Then I don't see him again until showtime the next night."

"When did you really understand there were these two people?"

"When I started directing in 1960, that's when I really started to understand it."

"Oh, when you were directing and also starring?"

He nodded again. "I was able to make the split. And I was able to understand things that weren't clear to me for so many years. Now I gotta get my shirt on."

"WHEN I WALK OUT ON THAT STAGE, I better sweat my balls off. That was my dad's training. If you don't sweat, you're not a pro. He always said that to me. If you don't sweat, you don't belong in this business. He said, 'Florsheim salesmen don't sweat.'"

"[I feel as if] tonight is the first time I've ever gone on stage in my life. And it's 59 years I've been doing that. But tonight, especially opening night, I drank that much blackberry brandy [half a glass], and I take a couple of Lomotil to settle my stomach, because there's nothing more embarrassing to be on the stage and feel like you've got the runs, okay! Or that you've got to pee! Nothing worse!"

"I have never sat down in my tux pants, never in my career."

"Now remember, comedy is also looked upon as slapstick. It's looked upon as lowbrow, as, well, who the hell can't do that. And how come it has no category [for an Academy Award]? Because the academy doesn't want to lower themselves to give an award to slapstick. They don't remember that the very thing that created the academy was the Keystone Cops. They waited until Chaplin was dying to give him an award. They waited until Stan Laurel was dying to give him an award. Don't wait until I die, folks. Let me have it now. Or just pat me on the head and give my work a category. The guy that invented the new subdiffused light for the men's room in theaters got a special Academy Award."

"Everyone that walks out on that stage is a child. They're out there for one reason—to get parental love and affection and understanding—and applause is, 'I love you, baby.' Applause is, 'Good job, sweetheart.'"

Richard Lewis

Photographing Richard Lewis turned out to be very cheap and convenient for me. He landed in my backyard twice in 1990. The first time was on July 4th, when he came to D.C. to promote his HBO special ("I'm Doomed") on "Larry King Live." He called me a few days before and said it was fine with him if I photographed him there, but to make sure to get the necessary permission from the show, which I took care of as soon as I hung up.

Richard once told me that the comedians he likes are the ones who are as funny off stage as they are on stage. He could have been describing himself. He was on a roll from the minute he hopped out of his limo and saw me being ejected from the lobby of the building where CNN is located. Richard had the security types laughing in no time, and we all rode up together in the elevator to the studio.

A member of the staff, who moments earlier had thrown me out without even listening to an explanation (apparently the show's publicist hadn't given her the word that I was coming), looked right past me and began fawning all over Richard, who hardly noticed. He was already into a stream-of-consciousness thing regaling the hair stylist and track star Carl Lewis, who was also a guest on the show and was wearing a silk suit that Richard kept saying was to die for.

A few weeks later I flew down to West Palm Beach to see Richard perform in concert at the Carefree Theater. Backstage before the show, I had a closeup look at Richard's show "notes." These consist of pages of yellow legal pad paper taped together with thousands of words of new material scribbled in longhand. It's his personal boa that he takes on stage with him for every performance. He told me that his only concern while on stage is that there's enough light to be able to reference his five feet of "notes."

Early in November, Richard was back in D.C. again to do a concert at Constitution Hall. I met him in his dressing room 45 minutes before the show, and after catching up on his latest adventures, I started shooting some pictures. It was getting close to showtime, and he began changing into his stage clothes. All of a sudden I did a double take and almost dropped the camera. I was stunned by the muscular definition of his physique. He had a new body. This wasn't the same Richard I saw without his shirt on in July at the Carefree Theater.

Shrugging nonchalantly, he asked if I really noticed a difference and said something about working out with a personal trainer for the past four months. As he left to go on stage, he did mention in passing that I'd be seeing him seminude in bed with Jamie Lee Curtis on an upcoming episode of "Anything but Love" and that he wasn't about to be mocked by her (or the crew, for that matter).

"I LOVE BEING A COMEDIAN because I have control over my own destiny, and that's why I went on stage to begin with. I wanted no one to shut me up. I wanted no one to judge me except the audience—not family or ex-girlfriends. And I wanted to speak louder than my family did around the table. So, I called all the shots."

"[Right before I go out on stage] it's chaos. It's chaos. Well, that's what my act is anyway, mainly because I don't know what I'm going to do, and I think, God, I haven't had a good bowel movement in about 40 years. And I haven't since Cuomo decided not to run."

"When an audience is hooked into my head, it's really one of the great thrills. I mean, I'm just like suspended animation. I don't think about the leak in my den. I don't think about any rashes. I just think that I'm making a couple thousand people laugh, and also, in a more indulgent way, having them laugh at things that are important to me. It's a thrill. And, of course, I'm filled with such low self-esteem that when they don't laugh, it almost is better for the act, because then it validates how I really feel about myself."

"I plan [coming off stage] generally well in advance. I have to go back to my bed as fast as possible. It's almost like the Indy 500 for a Jew."

"People become unnecessarily neurotic because they unthinkingly accept other people's perceptions of who they are, and I, for years, always felt defined by other people. So, basically, when I go on stage I say, 'I'm not crazy, they're crazy.'"

"I need to laugh when I feel someone's telling the truth. I just hate fabrication. I hate it in every facet of my life. Most of my friends are truthful, and most of my favorite comics are truthful. I just don't like lies. Of course, I'm lying to you right now, but other than that ...."

Steve Martin

I was introduced to Steve Martin on a chilly June night in Burbank, California, during an outdoor location shoot for his film *L.A. Story*. Since it was a closed set, I was grateful to be there and thanked Steve for having me. He in turn told me how much he liked my previous book, which impressed the hell out of me because: a) he'd actually looked through it, and b) he remembered it.

All through the long night, between takes, Steve would pedal his bike through the darkness back to his trailer about a quarter of a mile away. Since the ratio of time stars spend in their trailer versus the time they're on the set seems to be about 100 to 1, I had a lot of time to kill. But when Steve was on the set, all sorts of things happened. At one point a freeway sign lit up and was flashing messages on and off, a wind machine was blowing, and a beautiful full moon was hanging from a crane. They were doing a closeup telephoto shot of Steve and Victoria Tennant kissing, and the moon was supposed to be in the background right behind their heads. So, via the crane, they simply positioned a backlit model of a bright harvest moon (hanging from two wires) right where they wanted it and rolled the cameras for the perfect shot.

A few days later the filming moved to an indoor set in the Valley to shoot interiors. The day was blazing hot (116 degrees), and I was happy to spend time talking to Steve in his trailer. It was a regular oasis of air conditioning, soothing music, and refreshments (fruit, bottled water, and rice cakes). I was curious how, in his early days of doing stand-up, he (or any young comedian, for that matter) could really gauge how well he was doing. "When you see people who are watching you night after night, like the waiters and waitresses and the band, and they're laughing harder and harder, that's some kind of good sign," he explained.

A couple of weeks later, I photographed him on the set of *My Blue Heaven*, which was filming that day on a baseball field at Loyola-Marymount University. Steve thought it would be interesting for me to see him looking completely different, this time as a slick mobster with black hair standing straight up in a whiffle cut. He was right, especially in one scene where he launched into one of his patented "wild-and-crazy" dance numbers that broke up the cast, the crew, and the extras. Watching him do a number of takes of the dancing scene reminded me of something he told me about the effects of doing stand-up when he used to tour the country performing.

"I'd be on the road, and I'd do a show. Some nights I'd go home and feel great. And some nights I'd go home and really feel down. It took me years to figure out that it was exactly related to how the show went."

"BAD PAINTING IS STILL CALLED ART, but only great comedy is called art. Bad comedy is just terrible."

"Stand-up has a certain kind of anxiety connected with it, because the thing that makes it thrilling, the thing that eventually kills you, is that you are completely, 100 percent, entirely responsible. When I was doing my act and was hot, no one could ever tell me anything. They couldn't say, 'Don't do that joke tonight.' They couldn't say, 'I think you ought to start with this; our audience won't like that.' It was completely and always your decision."

"[In stand-up] you have to have visible confidence, authority, and the audience has to trust you. I think if they think you're worried, you're dead."

"In general, I think every comedian knows that you're only one inch away from disaster all the time."

"[Ten seconds before walking out on stage] I have a feeling that's identical to the feeling an athlete feels, say a football player at the kickoff, or when they announce his name, and he runs onto the field. It's a train leaving a station and you're on it."

"Playing for a large house was like doing a ballet, because every movement was—I'm not saying it's choreographed—it's made perfect. You're working from your fingernails to your toes for that kind of house. And eventually that's what made it for me. That was the joy of it. It was almost like you could be doing it alone, because it was something about your body, for me. The laughter was almost like it was part of the act. It was like, what do you do while they're laughing?"

"[After coming off stage] you were mostly exhausted, drenched. It was a very good feeling, because it was like having exercised, which I did. It was such a physical act. And on a good night, it felt like Stravinsky."

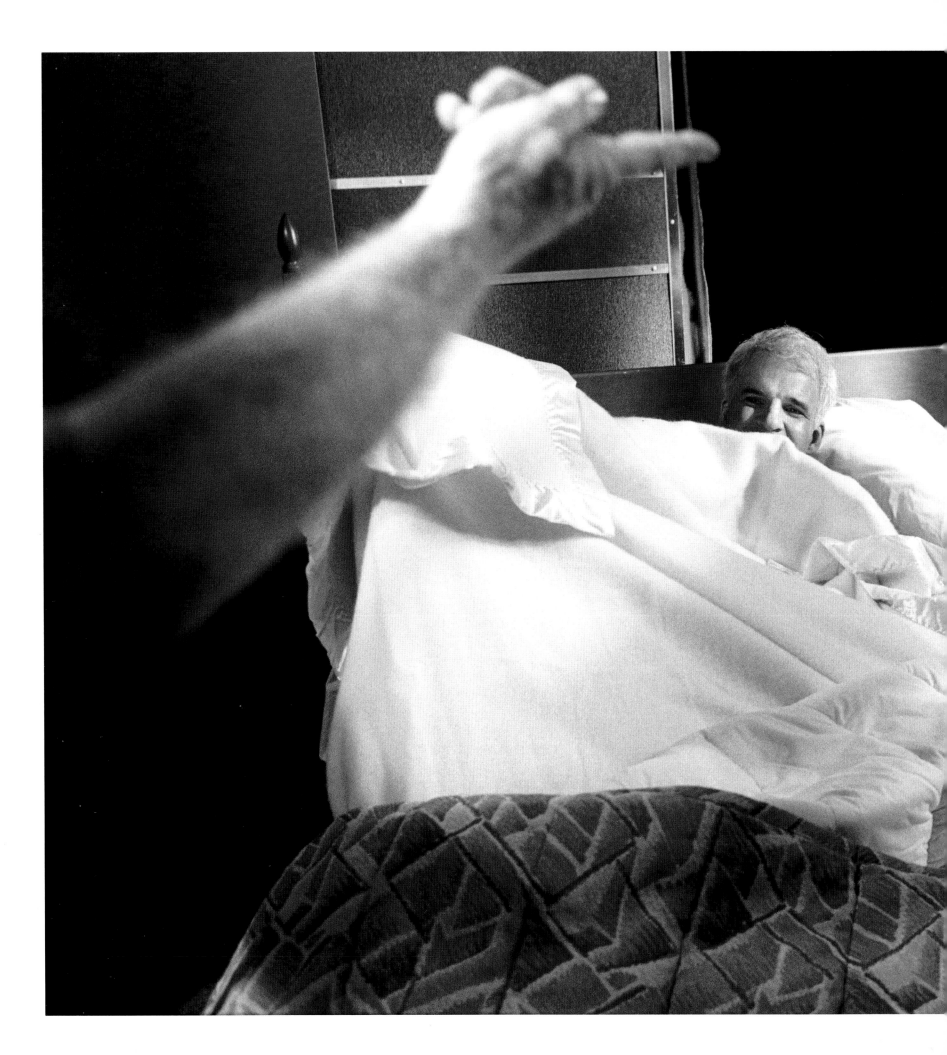

Jackie Mason

I met Jackie Mason for the first time in a deli. I'd just arrived at Resorts International Hotel in Atlantic City, and I called Jackie's suite to touch base and figure out when we would start shooting. I was told he was downstairs eating in one of the restaurants. Since it was brunch time, I headed straight for the deli, and there he was, seated with a group of his friends. The first words out of his mouth were, "Hi, have a seat. You're not a Jew, are you? You don't look like a Jew. What kind of name is Grace?"

Actually, it was a very pleasant brunch, with Jackie holding court, delivering one funny line after another. Afterward, a few of us went up to Jackie's suite to watch a championship boxing match. He's a major fan, and during the fight, he got right up and threw punches at the screen as if he were in the ring with the fighters. When the fight was over, he started working the telephone (which he seemed to do constantly), and I left.

Late in the afternoon, all of us went over to the newly refurbished Showboat Hotel because Jackie wanted to check it out. We soon found ourselves in the coffee shop around a table of "comped" food. I decided this would be a good time for an interview, so I pulled out my pocket tape recorder. This was my first attempt at one of these Q & A's, and I really hadn't yet formulated a standard set of questions. However, a very good friend of mine who's married to a comedian suggested that I

would get an interesting response if I asked every comedian how they felt about death. It seemed like an interesting idea, so I tried it on Jackie.

AG: How do you feel about death?

JM: Good. In your case, perfect. Very good for you. Two more questions like this, and I'll see to it myself.

Everybody gathered again in Jackie's dressing room backstage before the show. It was pretty low-key, as Jackie went over some new material he was going to try out that night. When it was ten minutes to showtime, he went into his changing room to get dressed. I wasn't paying attention to the time, but the next thing I knew, the stage manager came running in looking for Jackie. She opened the door to his room, and there he was, dozing in his chair facing the makeup mirror. He woke right up, dashed off, and was on stage getting laughs within 30 seconds.

The next time I saw him was in Los Angeles at the Henry Fonda Theater. He was in tryouts with *Brand New*, the second one-man show he was going to bring to Broadway. The highlight of the night was watching Jackie schmooze backstage with comedian Jan Murray and then listening to Jackie's theory why it's only snob appeal that separates a New York beach from a beach on the French Riviera. "It's the same sand. If you put it in a jar, would you know where it came from?"

"IT'S A LOT EASIER TO FIND an exceptionally good opera singer than a great comedian because there are very, very few great comedians."

"[Before I go out on stage] what really goes through my mind is a sense of anticipation, a readiness to go and be a hit, a desire to please, a feeling of responsibility toward that audience. But I don't have too much insecurity or concern about it, because I have no doubt that I will be a hit by the time the show is over. I feel like a guy who knows how to be a diamond cutter. He doesn't get nervous in front of every diamond. He knows his business, and he knows he can do it well. Maybe if it's a little more expensive diamond, he'll get a little nervous he could make a mistake. But listen, a brain surgeon gets a little nervous too. But the best brain surgeons don't get that nervous, because they know if the guy passes away, that's his problem."

"[When I walk off stage] I appreciate the fact that I was just a big hit. Because I almost always am. And I feel comfortable. Sometimes if I don't feel I'm as big a hit as I could have been, I feel a little disturbed about it. Because I'm a great perfectionist about my work . . . but it's worth it, because it's a great challenge to constantly struggle to be a hit."

"The older Jews are embarrassed by anything Jewish and always subconsciously feel that if it's Jewish, it can't succeed because the gentiles don't like the Jew and you should avoid your Jewishness because you won't be acceptable. And all of a sudden, they find a Jew who is so pronouncedly Jewish not only accepted, but heralded by all the gentile critics and all the opinion makers and thinkers of this country. They had to find out from the gentiles that I'm a hit."

Richard Pryor

"[RIGHT BEFORE I WENT OUT ON STAGE, I thought] I hope I'm funny.   I hope I make 'em laugh, and they enjoy it. Yeah, the numbers came easy, you know.   Like one, two, three, four, five, six, seven, eight, nine, ten. I mean it came like that. There was times when if you was on the numbers, you know, you'd be in the time. Time and space, you controlled it."

"[Coming off stage] I would have a high. I remember that. I had a high, and it would take awhile to come down, you know. And I usually liked to be alone, go somewhere, just in a room, just face the wall or something. Yeah, that was a most wonderful feeling in the world for me. I mean you couldn't touch me with a long stick. No, I was somewhere else. I don't know where, but I was there, wherever there is."

"[What I brought to comedy—] I think the honesty. Yeah, I think just saying, put your feelings out there. I don't think they did that before."

"I see Laurel and Hardy up there with van Gogh. I do, really. Cause they were just there, man, you know what I'm saying. They had a love. They had a magic together."

"I like them [stand-up comedians] to laugh. I like that they like it, and they work hard at it. I think I respect that the most. The men and the women, I really enjoy the labor they put in. I know how hard it is and how they make it look so easy and that makes me happy. And I like it when they take the chance. If they don't take the chance, what they doin' it for?"

I wasn't able to photograph Richard Pryor until October 1990, because he was recuperating from a mild heart attack he'd suffered earlier in the year on a trip to Australia. We finally met in Manhattan on the set of *Another You*, a comedy he was costarring in with Gene Wilder. He was surrounded by a tight coterie of people who had great respect and affection for him, including his longtime hair stylist and makeup artist.

The director on the picture at that time (but later replaced) was Peter Bogdanovich. He would glide around the set with a bottled water in one hand, checking last-minute details before the cameras rolled. He was always jawing with Richard, with his non–bottled water hand on Richard's shoulder, talking into his ear, at various times giving advice, instruction, or encouragement. But more often than not, he was practicing his highly acclaimed skills as a raconteur. Richard, who is in a class by himself when it comes to telling funny stories, would listen politely, sometimes with a strained look on his face, never quite sure where the story was headed or where the punch line was.

I had a chance to talk to Richard briefly one afternoon in his trailer as he was being made up for his next scene. We were discussing stand-up, and I asked him what he felt was the most difficult part of being a stand-up comedian. "Having 12 wives," he answered immediately. Then he went on to say that he never saw anything difficult about it and never perceived it that way. As far as the differences between doing film comedy and doing stand-up were concerned—"Stand-up's the best," he said without hesitation. "Yeah, 'cause you go home and you know. You know right there actually. Yeah, the first 30 seconds."

A few days later the filming had moved to an outdoor location for a street scene. Richard was dressed down for the shot and fit right in with the people in the neighborhood. Still, he drew a crowd during the short walk from his trailer to the set across the street, and people shouted his name from passing cars and nearby windows. Everybody acted as if he were one of them, and that's exactly how Richard acted. When I left that day, I asked him how he felt about being a comedian, and he said he took great pride in it. But then he quickly added, "*And* it pays for the kids and the wives."

Joan Rivers

"TIMING IS A GIFT from the gods. You can't learn timing."

"[I'm thinking right before I go on stage] is my bra showing? I'm so egocentric. Do I look okay? No, the last thing that goes through your mind, truthfully, is how are they? Because I always ask the opening act as they come off. It's the last thing I hear contact-wise with anybody before I hit the stage. That gives you indications for how hard you're going to have to work that night—if it's going to be a party or if it's going to be work. Then you go out prepared."

"Let me just tell you something. This is a business that is an asexual business. If my dog, Spike, has 15 good minutes, he would be a star. Do you understand? If Hitler came back with half an hour of strong material, he would be a star. It has nothing to do with men and women."

"[Comedy's] a very strong field. You have to be a very strong person to work in it. You can't be a Marilyn Monroe on stage. You're a lion tamer out there, and you've got to carry a chair and a whip."

"I never rest on my laurels. Constantly working on the act. Constantly updating the act. Constantly making it current. Constantly offending somebody. Because the minute you don't offend somebody, that means you're off the edge. If you're off the edge, you're moving onto a level."

"I was the first one that brought the truth about women's feelings on stage—absolute truth—and discussed really what women think and really what women are feeling. The first one ever to do that. Because up to then nobody ever really told the truth. I talked about having an affair with a married man. You just didn't talk about that. I talked about women's problems—having a baby, going to a gynecologist, douching, faking orgasm—all that. I was the first one ever to bring it to the stage—good, bad, or indifferent."

I began photographing Joan Rivers in late February 1990 at CBS Studios on 57th Street in Manhattan, where on weekdays she does her syndicated talk show, "The Joan Rivers Show." At the time, she was taping two shows a day, which isn't exactly easy to pull off. There are guest briefings to read, questions to prepare, jokes to write, and wardrobe changes to make—all within a limited amount of time. I could see right away, as I got caught up in the backstage whirlwind, that the lazy and the faint of heart need not apply for Joan's job.

Her dressing room buzzed with activity as she decided on clothes, accessories, and hair styles at the same time she worked on the next show's script with her producers and writers. And all the while, there was Spike, her trusty Yorkshire terrier, keeping watch over his mistress' domain (which meant he kept barking like crazy at any stranger who came near Joan). Amidst all of this, I was introduced to Joan and immediately receded into the background. What I remember most vividly was the intricate choreography between Joan's hair stylist, makeup man, and wardrobe assistant. They took her from lounging robe to stage-ready in what seemed like only moments.

I met Joan again some months later in Las Vegas where she was doing an engagement at Caesar's Palace. She flew in from New York after taping her show, arrived early in the evening, and went right to her dressing room. I found out from her manager that even though they were doing two shows that night, they were flying right back to New York by private jet after the second show so they could attend the daytime Emmy awards (Joan's talk show had been nominated).

Twice that night I watched Joan prepare both mentally and physically to take the stage before a packed house and then each time deliver over an hour of demanding comedy. In between shows, she changed back into her robe and had some quiet time to relax and sleep. But as soon as the curtain came down on her second show at 1:15 A.M., with Spike under her arm, she headed for the airport and the flight to Manhattan. I was completely exhausted at that point, but Joan was still on the move.

Later the next afternoon, as I was sitting by the hotel pool, Joan was already in the air chasing the sun back to Las Vegas for that night's performance, with Spike and her new Emmy in tow.

Lily Tomlin

"I'VE HAD A LOT MORE FREEDOM and success and everything else working by myself. First of all, I like to, as a form. As a young girl, I always loved somebody creating something out of nothing, just with their voice and their body. I found it much more exciting. I would be transported."

"Nerves you have mostly at opening night, and then you have nerves if you know somebody special is in the audience. What makes you able to really be consistently good is that if you play to a thousand people and 999 don't appreciate what you're doing, you'd always believe there's one person you have to do it right for."

"I've heard stories [that] the stand-up comic is like the most courageous, most dangerous. I don't know. It depends. So if you bomb, you bomb. Once you get used to bombing, had the experience, you just have it. All you have to do is just share that you're bombing."

"You'd look like a real fool doing comedy or satirizing something if you didn't have any sense of humor about yourself. What you deal in is people's behavior and people's weaknesses."

"There's something significant, talking about men and women in comedy. It's just that thing of standing up and being in control—daring to take control of a group of people. First of all, very few women see themselves in that role, consciously or not. They just don't. To make people laugh is to be powerful, because people are vulnerable when they laugh . . . and women are not supposed to be powerful."

"I personally don't think I'm that funny. I think I know what's funny. I think what's made me successful has been my selectivity in material. Instead of commenting on this week, I comment on this decade, I guess."

When the elevator doors opened on the fifth floor of Cincinnati's Westin Hotel, there was Lily Tomlin. We were both on our way down to meet each other for a late-night drink in the lobby bar. She had just returned from the theater, where she was starring in Jane Wagner's *The Search for Signs of Intelligent Life in the Universe*. Over a hot chocolate, a glass of champagne, and a cucumber sandwich, she talked about her early days as a stand-up. Or to be accurate, as Lily pointed out, "In real life I never was a stand-up, but I had the guts to stand up [alone] for some reason."

The next time I saw Lily was in April at the Wilshire Theater in Los Angeles. I arrived in the afternoon in time to watch her rehearse for that evening's performance of *Search*. She's a perfectionist in her work and a consummate professional, and I was amazed as I watched her tweak and fine-tune aspects of her performance which would seem irrelevant or invisible to a general audience. However, the quality of the end result was such that Meryl Streep went backstage after that evening's show to compliment Lily, genuinely and enthusiastically, on her work.

The following evening I had a chance to talk to Lily in her dressing room before the show. She was sitting with Tess, a Norwich terrier who travels with her everywhere. We were discussing the subject of women in comedy, and she told me a story about how years ago when she was working at the Upstairs in New York, there was a very pretty girl in the revue who was dull on stage but hysterically funny in the dressing room telling stories in character. Lily told her she ought to be performing that material on stage. However, the girl would then "pull herself up—literally, her hair would kind of electrify—and she'd get all kind of perfect and pretty again and she'd say, 'I wouldn't want anyone to think I was unattractive.'" Lily said this girl was a perfect example of the widely held belief that somehow, if a woman did stand-up, she would lose her femininity.

During the summer, I photographed Lily again at San Francisco's Golden Gate Theater. She had already completed the film version of *Search* and was briefly staging the play again in case they needed further live shots or exteriors to weave into the movie. Nothing had changed at rehearsal. Lily was still spending hours going over changes, cues, and sound levels. Later that night, after playing to another sold-out house, she took Tess for a walk in a nearby park, then went back to her hotel and worked on her film at an elaborate portable editing system she had set up in her suite. As I walked back to my hotel at 1:30 in the morning, I remembered mentioning to Lily how accessible comedians seemed to be compared to other performers. "I suppose people would be more nervous approaching Elizabeth Taylor than me," she remarked. "They see me, and they think they see a friend."

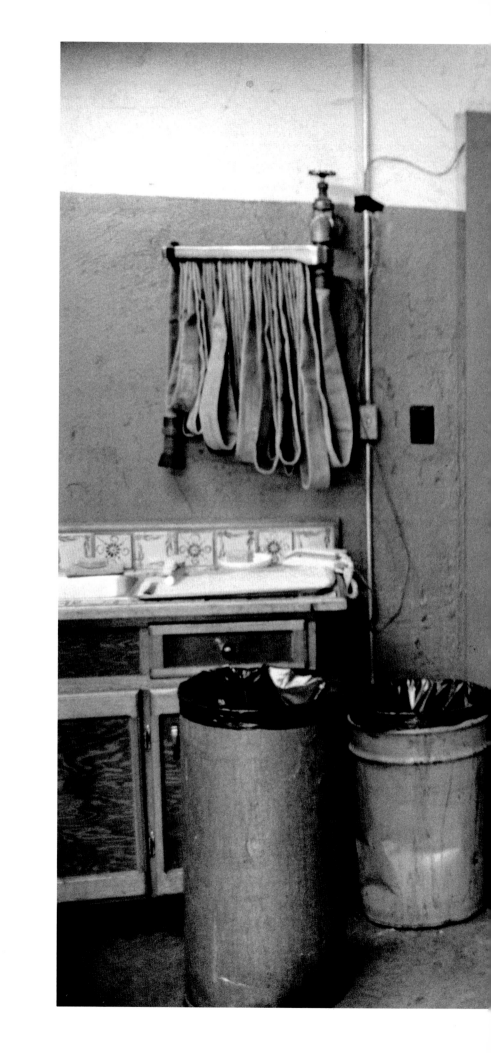

Robin Williams

Although I worked with Robin Williams on film sets in 1990 (*Cadillac Man* and *The Fisher King*), I especially wanted to photograph him during Comic Relief week when he'd be doing live comedy on stage. I arrived in New York on a Wednesday afternoon and went right over to the rehearsal room at Radio City where Robin, Billy, and Whoopi, as well as assorted writers, producers, and managers, were busy hashing out the show. Ideas, both good and bad, were flying around the room, and when the funny ones hit, you could see that the creative process, although messy at times, certainly had its moments.

The next day Robin went to wardrobe to be fitted for his costume for the Siegfried and Roy tiger-taming skit. The blond wig was divine, but the satin jacket with tails was a size too small and the pants were so tight he turned to the tailor and commented that the audience wouldn't have any trouble figuring out what religion he was. Then he went into an Elvis impersonation, swinging his hips and cocking his lip, doing Elvis as Siegfried the fearless wild animal trainer to the delight of the enthralled seamstresses.

The next night we went out to the Mets game for Comic Relief at Shea Stadium. There was a good-sized crowd waiting for Robin when the car pulled up, and once he got out, it turned into a scene from the Beatles movie *A Hard Day's Night*, with Robin's fans starting to mob him for autographs. His publicist, Mark Rutenberg, took control and, with some police help, hustled Robin into a security guard's office with the crowds chasing behind and waving their paper and pens. The guard inside the tiny cubicle jerked his head up from his paperwork as the door slammed shut. He did a double take, then blurted out, "Hey, man, you're Robin Williams! Gimme your autograph!" (If you're a celebrity, this must be your vision of hell.)

I saw Robin a few months later in Los Angeles, where he was on location for the movie *The Fisher King*. He was taking some sun with his blue-tongued lizard on the beach in Malibu during a break in filming. Nearby was a beautiful white cockatoo in a five-foot cage, a recent birthday present. The waves were starting to build, so it seemed like a good idea to go body-surfing. He donned his "frog" gloves (for extra speed) and headed in. After half a dozen good rides and accompanying poundings on the shoreline, he walked uncomfortably back to his towel, complaining that he had sand in places he didn't know you could get sand into.

Later, as he was drying off, I asked Robin what some of the problems were in doing film comedy versus stand-up. He thought for a second and quipped, "A year's a long time to wait for a laugh."

"THERE'S A LOT OF PEOPLE THAT MAKE ME LAUGH. Henry Kissinger makes me laugh. I make myself laugh when I'm nude in front of the mirror, pointing out where I've been. Bebe Rebozo makes me laugh. Just the name, Bebe Rebozo. Sounds like a bad Vegas act."

"[As an art form, comedy rates] somewhere between ballet and door-to-door salesman, although the French consider it an art form. But they also consider pastry an art form."

"In Plato's discussion of comedy, it was designed to make fun, to deflate, because it basically makes us realize we're human. It makes people realize that you do trip, we fall, we fart, we touch ourselves. We have foibles. And that's all the strange things that make man man, and make it wonderful but also funny. We are man, we are incredible. Yeah, but you still smell."

"Talking seriously about comedy is like a clown wearing lead-based makeup. It's like breaking a joke down. When you actually start to ask why do the two Jews walk into the bar, it's not funny anymore."

"[What's going through my head ten seconds before I go on stage is] my bowels, and the incredible need to move them to Cleveland. To get them somewhere else. To rent out my bowels. Suddenly urinate. To go where every man has gone! To yawn, feel my head, to suddenly collapse, to leave my body, to have a Shirley MacLaine experience without the guy with a voice that sounds like he has a vibrator in his throat! Go! To go beyond myself! To leave this world, this planet; to stand outside my body and watch somebody else die! These are the things—yeah, ten seconds before you go on, I get—there's a thing that happens with reverse nerves. I get very sleepy, almost narcoleptic!"

"[What I do is] scat comedy. The ability to have no act, the quilt school of comedy, to bring back that sense of not knowing where you're going! Like being with Ray Charles in the wilderness, that kind of thing. I mean, what I remember is just free-forming again, like Jonathan [Winters] did."

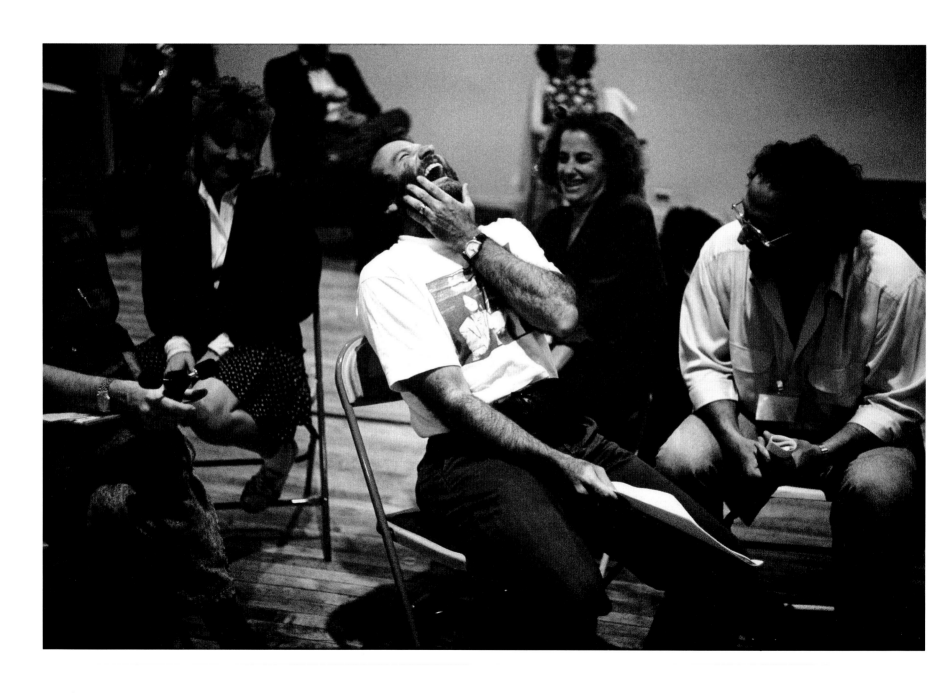

Steven Wright

"I THINK IT [STAND-UP] is the most difficult form of show business, not just comedy. You write it yourself, you decide where to say what joke, when to stop, bang, bang, everything. It's live. You can't stop it and say you want to start again because I'm not flowing here, let's cut. If the sound goes, you're screwed. You get in trouble, you're in trouble. There's no turning back. It's just you. You get all the glory, but you take all that's going wrong."

"[Right before I go out] it's like I'm thinking of going to meet these people, and I'm hoping it's a good connection. It's like you're connecting your mind to their mind. All the commotion is over, and now it's time for us to have this weird meeting. I'm not nervous. I'm just anxious, because as many years as I've been doing it, I still think it is a strange thing to do—one guy to talk to that many people."

"The stage is strange. The rules are different. Time can go faster or slower. Everything you say, every move you make, is magnified. So you're anxious, because you're going into the arena like a bullfighter. The stakes are all higher. It's like this little magic land. If you get them laughing, it's an incredible rush. If they don't laugh at something, it's uncomfortable to have 2,000 people looking at you when you said something that you obviously thought was funny and 2,000 people say we don't agree by their silence. And you have to be able to deal with that. The silence of 2,000 people is a lot of silence."

"[When I come off stage] I'm back now. It's like a kite. You were up there, and now you're down, and you're kind of like still tingling from the experience. It's almost like you came out of the rain into a house, and you are still wet. There's still water on you, and in two minutes you're going to be dry, and it's going to be like you weren't there at all."

I had no trouble spotting Steven Wright the first time I met him. He was walking through the lobby of Omaha, Nebraska's Red Lion Hotel, wearing his hometown Boston Red Sox baseball cap. He was in the middle of a Midwest concert tour, traveling from city to city by private bus. When I asked him how long a drive he had to make to his next date in Ohio (thinking I might try to tag along), there was an ominous pause before he blithely informed me it was a 17-hour trip. (I flew home the next day.)

When we arrived at the theater early that evening, there were a few surprises. The dressing room was big enough for a chorus line, and there was an actual, real-live, three-ring circus going on in an adjacent part of the complex. After going over some notes and playing his guitar for a while, Steve headed for the stage area. As he waited for the crowd to take their seats after the intermission, he started talking about the stage and how different types of performers made their living on it. Dancers, for instance, were so physical. "But all I need my body for is to carry my brain out there," he noted.

When we returned to the hotel, the lobby area was awash with evening gowns and military uniforms. A local R.O.T.C. ball was in full swing, and people kept coming up to Steven, shaking his hand, complimenting him, and asking him to pose for pictures. Always polite, but somewhat bewildered by it all, he finally ducked into the elevator and headed for his room.

A half-hour later, we met for a late dinner in the ground floor coffee shop, which was located in an open area off the lobby next to one of the ballrooms. Within moments somebody walked up to the table and said, "Hi Steve, remember me? I met you the last time you were in Omaha. We were up in the bar on the 19th floor of the hotel when the tornado hit. Remember?" Steve shook his head in a noncommittal way, and the man soon left. Steve said he had no idea what the guy was talking about, but that the drinks in the rooftop bar must have been something else. Next, a young couple approached Steve to tell him how much they liked him and went on to say, without any prompting, that they had driven from Chicago to Omaha for the weekend just to check out a band they wanted to hire for their wedding the following year. Steve remarked that it seemed like a long way to go to find a band.

Finally, an R.O.T.C. officer came up to shake Steve's hand, and as he turned to leave, he asked Steve to make sure and let him know if he heard of any good wars. By this time the scene was getting to be too much, and Steve, looking slightly perplexed, gave his thoughts on the matter in his own inimitable style. "You know, I wanted to sit in this restaurant so I could watch all the people walk by. The only thing I didn't realize is that they could see me too."

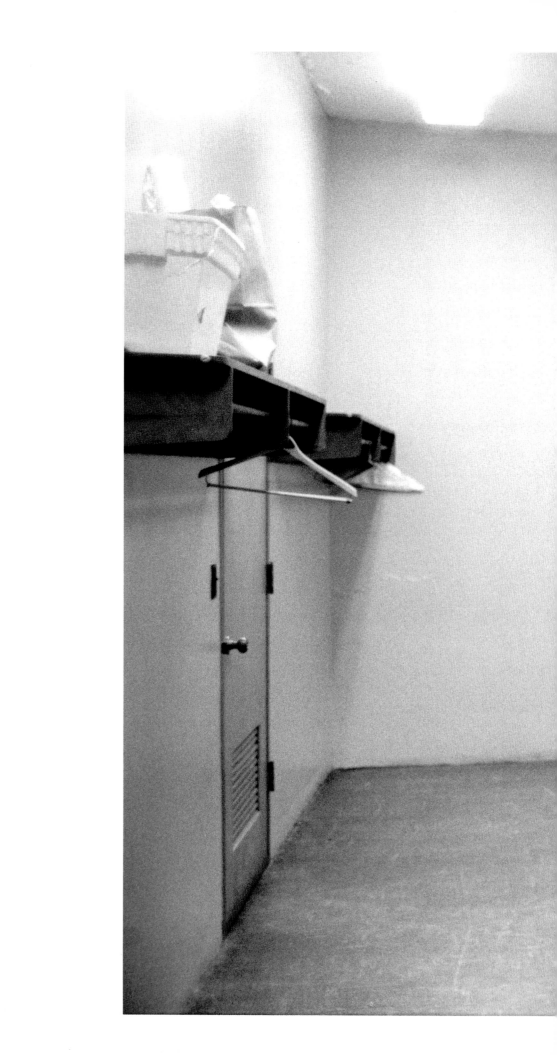

Acknowledgements

Special thanks to Raymond DeMoulin and the Professional Photography Division of Eastman Kodak Company for their support.

I would also like to thank: Eliane Laffont of Sygma photo agency for her tireless efforts on behalf of this project; Jane Livingston for her artistic guidance and insightful photographic editing; Alex Castro for his inspired design and unerring advice; Bill Pierce for his exquisite photographic printing and steadfast friendship; and Paul Mahon of Lowe and Mahon for his wise counsel.

Also my thanks to Larry Brezner, Buddy Morra, David Steinberg, and Linda Kwasha who were instrumental in getting this project off the ground.

On the technical side, I would like to acknowledge the generous assistance of Rollei Fototechnic, and specifically, U.S. representatives Roger Bartzke and Bob Solomon. Their Rolleiflex cameras once again performed flawlessly.

Special thanks also to Ken Hansen of Ken Hansen Photographic for his unflinching and generous support at all times.

Others who deserve my thanks and were most helpful at various times and in various ways include: *Life* magazine director of photography Peter Howe, David Fisher, Mark Rutenberg, Rich Clarkson, Dick Bagdasarian of Pro Photo in Washington, D.C., Judith Hendra, Joe Aprea, Ralph Alswang, Eugene Pierce, Jerry Hamza, Irving Fein, Paul Bloch, Arnold Lipsman, Michelle Marx, Dorothy Melvin, Rory Rosegarten, Lisa Traina, Judy Van Herpen, Ward Grant, Ron Holder, Tom Gray, Joe Stabile, Tim Sarkas, and Guy McElwaine.

Also, I would like to thank those who have not previously been mentioned who kindly took the time to be interviewed for this book: Marty Klein, Bernie Brillstein, Jack Rollins, Mitzi Shore, Bud Friedman, and Howard Klein.

Finally, I am most grateful to all the comedians who participated in this project and would like to thank them for their kindness, generosity, and trust. I hope this book lives up to their expectations.

And of course, I can't forget Buster and Tetley, who always calmed me down when people didn't return my phone calls.

ABOUT THE AUTHOR

Arthur Grace began his photographic career in 1972 with United Press International. Over the past 19 years, he has covered stories throughout the U.S. and abroad as a contract photographer for *Time* and most recently as a staff photographer at *Newsweek*. Through his affiliation with Sygma photo agency, his photographs regularly appear in leading publications worldwide. Grace is also the author of *Choose Me: Portraits of a Presidential Race*. He lives with his wife, Florence, outside of Washington, D.C., and is currently freelancing and working on a new book.